21st Century Skills Library

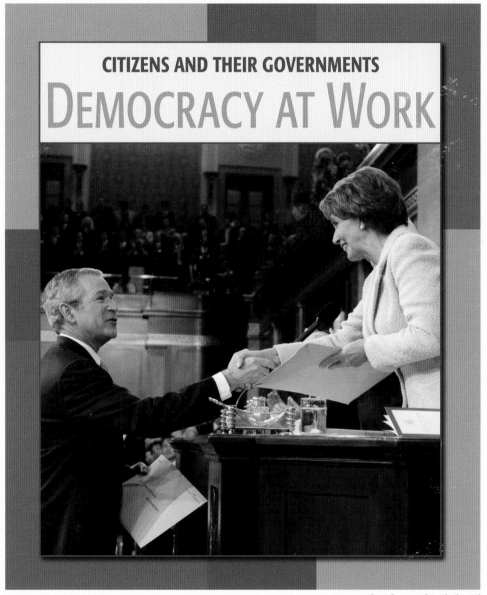

CITIZENS AND THEIR GOVERNMENTS

DEMOCRACY AT WORK

Fredrik Liljeblad

Cherry Lake Publishing
Ann Arbor, Michigan

CHERRY LAKE
Publishing

Published in the United States of America by Cherry Lake Publishing
Ann Arbor, MI
www.cherrylakepublishing.com

Cover, © Larry Downing/Pool/CNP/CORBIS; Title Page, © Larry Downing/Pool/
CNP/CORBIS; Page 8, Photo Courtesy of Library of Congress; Page 16, © Yuri Gripas/
Reuters/CORBIS; Page 19, © Bettmann/CORBIS; Page 20, Photo Courtesy of Library
of Congress; Page 21, © Shepard Sherbell/CORBIS; Page 22, Photo Courtesy of LBJ
Library; Page 24, © Collection, The Supreme Court Historical Society, Steve Petteway

Library of Congress Cataloging-in-Publication Data
Liljeblad, Fredrik, 1952-
  Democracy at work/by Fredrik Liljeblad.
     p. cm.—(Citizens and their government)
  Includes bibliographical references and index.
  ISBN-13: 978-1-60279-058-2 (alk. paper)
  ISBN-10: 1-60279-058-2 (alk. paper)
  1. United States—Politics and government—Juvenile literature. I. Title.
II. Series.
  JK40.L55 2008
  320.473—dc22   2007006077

*Cherry Lake Publishing would like to acknowledge the work of
The Partnership for 21st Century Skills.
Please visit* www.21stcenturyskills.org *for more information.*

TABLE OF CONTENTS

CHAPTER ONE

DEMOCRACY THEN AND NOW

Independence Hall is such a popular tourist site now that the park service provides information brochures in nine languages.

The Constitution of the United States is the foundation of American democracy. It was written in 1787 in Philadelphia, Pennsylvania. That's the reason Philadelphia and its Independence Hall are often called "the Cradle of Liberty."

The United States of America is the world's oldest democracy today. Other old democracies include Switzerland, which began in 1848. Canada became a democracy in 1867, and Australia became one in 1901. As you can see, the United States is by far the oldest.

The First Democracy

The United States wasn't the world's first democracy, however. In ancient Greece, the city-state

In the Greece of Pericles, only some people—men— could vote. Why would that policy not work in today's United States?

of Athens created the first democracy in about 500 B.C. The English word *democracy* is thought to come from the ancient Greek word *demokratia,* meaning "people-power."

A man named Pericles ruled Athens from about 462 B.C. to 429 B.C. He made several reforms that advanced democracy there. Scholars today call this the "golden age" of Greek democracy.

Athenian democracy wasn't like American democracy, however. For one thing, in Athens only adult male citizens with Athenian parents could vote. No men with foreign parents or any women—even if they were rich—could take part.

The Parthenon and other buildings on the Acropolis in Athens held meetings of leaders and the public.

Athenian voters gathered about 40 times a year at the "Speaker's Stone." There they decided on laws and other important issues such as war and taxes. This was a **direct democracy** because all voters were free to attend and decide on issues themselves.

Our Democracy

The United States is a **representative democracy**. There are way too many of us to assemble in one place. In fact, more than 117 million Americans voted in the 2004 presidential election. Instead, we elect small groups of people to represent our wishes. We elect mayors, council people,

In the early 1900s, thousands of people marched in New York City and elsewhere in favor of the right to vote for women.

and governors. We also elect senators, representatives, and a president. How often we elect people depends on local, state, and national laws. For example, we elect a president every four years.

Today, all citizens age 18 or older can vote. However, this was not always so. At first, only white males who owned property could vote. More than half a century later, African American males got the vote, as a result of the Civil War. It wasn't until 1920 that women could vote. This should have been the end of the United States' voting problems, but it wasn't.

Just because people had the right to vote didn't mean that in certain areas, some other people might

Learning & Innovation Skills

Many groups keep a close eye on voting to make sure it is fair. For example, poll taxes were outlawed when the 24th Amendment to the Constitution became law. Unfortunately, in our history other groups have sought to take advantage of the voting system. Why would they want to do that?

Learning & Innovation Skills

Requirements for voting and other guidelines were left to the states by the U.S. Constitution. As with other things, however, as times changed the Constitution was amended. Do you think it is a good thing to be able to change the Constitution? Why or why not?

not try to stop them. This was especially true in Southern states after the Civil War. White people there often tried to keep black people from voting. Many Southern states passed poll tax laws. These laws kept African Americans from voting, and the laws were not changed until 1964. Then thousands of African Americans proudly voted for the first time in their lives.

A Government that Shares Power

The men who wrote the U.S. Constitution did not want the government of the United States to turn out like that of England. They thought that King George III of England was a **tyrant**. These

"Founding Fathers" of the United States didn't want any one person or group to have that much power. As a result, they divided the government into three branches.

The three branches of our national government are the **legislative, executive,** and **judicial.** All three branches meet in Washington, D.C.

Each branch has certain powers that neither of the other two does. This system is called the **separation of powers.** It makes sure that no one branch is too powerful. It is the way that the Founding Fathers kept the United States from getting a too powerful "King George."

CHAPTER TWO

CONGRESS AND THE PRESIDENT

Congress meets in the U.S. Capitol Building in Washington, D.C.
George Washington laid the building's cornerstone in 1793.

Congress is the legislative branch of the federal government. It has two

parts. One part is the **Senate**. There are two senators from each state.

The other part of Congress is the **House of Representatives**. There are

435 representatives. Every state has at least one representative. However,

that only accounts for 50! The rest of the

representatives are distributed according to the

population of a state. The bigger the population is,

the greater the number of representatives.

Members of the Senate and the House of

Representatives play much the same role. They are

all elected to represent the people of their state.

They meet with people from their state and listen

to concerns. They meet with experts on agriculture,

science, education, foreign affairs, and other fields.

They use what they learn to make decisions about

new laws for the nation.

Representatives in Congress—in fact all government workers—are *accountable* to the people. What does the word "accountable" mean? What are you accountable for—and to whom?

In 1800, President John Adams and his family became the first occupants of the White House.

The Presidency

The president of the United States is one of the most powerful people in the world. In fact, many would claim that the president is the most powerful. The president deals with foreign governments and is commander-in-chief of the armed forces. The president does this to keep the country safe. At the start of each presidential term in office, the president swears an oath to "protect and defend" the United States of America.

The president also oversees the running of the federal government and appoints many officials. These many officials themselves oversee everything from the national parks and the U.S. military to NASA and the FBI. They control public health agencies such as the National Institutes of Health and the Centers for Disease Control and Prevention. They manage other groups such as the U.S. Mint, where our money is made, and the National Archives, where the U.S. Constitution is kept.

CHAPTER THREE

How Laws Are Made

*Members of Congress, such as Senator Lindsey Graham
shown on right, often meet with people, such as
Judge Samuel Alito, in their offices.*

Working Together

Although they play different roles, Congress and the president work

together to make new laws for the nation. Members of Congress meet

with citizens, specialists, and one another to find out what new laws might

be needed. They may meet with the president, too. It usually takes many

months of work to create a new law. Sometimes it takes years!

21st CENTURY SKILLS LIBRARY

Only senators or representatives can start the process for making a new law. However, the process can begin in either the Senate or the House. The senator or representative first writes up a **bill**. This document is assigned a number and sent to the proper committee. If the bill started in the Senate, it goes to a Senate committee. If the bill started in the House, it goes to a House committee.

Congressional committees have staff members help them work out the details of proposed laws.

Both the House and the Senate have many committees, and the bill will be sent to the proper one. For example, if the bill is about farming, it goes to the Agriculture Committee. If the bill is about spending money, it goes to the **Appropriations** Committee. However, most committees have many sub-committees too. For example, the Senate Committee on Appropriations has a dozen sub-committees. Most bills are sent directly from committees to sub-committees.

The sub-committee is made up of a small group of either senators or representatives. Some people on the sub-committee may be in favor of the bill. Others may be opposed.

Usually, the sub-committee will hold **hearings**. These are public sessions where experts and citizens are invited to speak to the sub-committee about the bill. These hearings may last several hours, or they may last several days.

Committee meetings are still sometimes as crowded as this 1929 Senate meeting on taxes was.

The U.S. Capitol Building has many committee meeting rooms as well as special chambers for the House and Senate.

Often the sub-committee will make **amendments** to the bill before

sending it back to the whole committee. If the committee agrees the bill is

ready, it is sent to the whole Senate or House. However, many bills never

get this far. Too many people have decided the bill is a bad idea. And hundreds or even thousands of bills are submitted every year. In fact, 341 new bills were submitted in just five days in October of 2006!

The bill is then carefully considered by the whole House or Senate. More amendments may be made. Then a vote is taken. If the vote is favorable, the bill is sent to the other chamber of Congress for consideration. If the other chamber also votes in favor of the bill, it is ready to be sent to the president.

Members of the House of Representatives have voted on these electronic voting machines since the late 1970s.

In 1965, President Lyndon Johnson signed the bill creating Medicare, a program that provides health insurance for older Americans.

The bill must be accepted or rejected by the president. If the president approves of the bill, he or she will sign it. Sometimes, these signing ceremonies are big affairs. Other times, the president just quietly signs the bill. However, the president can refuse to sign a bill. Such an action is called a **veto,** a Latin word meaning "I forbid."

A vetoed bill goes back to Congress. Then Congress can do one of three things. First, Congress can drop the bill. Second, Congress can try to change the bill to address the president's objections. Third, Congress can vote to **override** the president's veto. An override is a new vote in both the Senate and the House in which two-thirds of the members vote in favor of the bill. This strong vote in favor of a bill makes it a law.

Some presidents veto lots of bills and others very few. Warren G. Harding vetoed six bills, while Franklin Roosevelt vetoed 635. Why do you think Roosevelt may have vetoed so many bills? Hint: Think about what was happening during these presidents' terms.

CHAPTER FOUR

THE SUPREME COURT

Supreme Court justices usually have been judges in other U.S. courts
before they are chosen for the highest court in the land.

The Supreme Court is the third branch of the federal government. It

is also the highest court in the United States. There are nine justices on the court. Each justice is appointed by the president

and must be approved by the Senate. The Senate

holds hearings. Usually the proposed justice spends

several hours answering questions from senators

during these hearings. Other people, both those in

favor of the new appointment and those opposed,

will speak, too. Often this process takes several

months. Everyone wants to be very careful about who

becomes a justice of the Supreme Court because each

one holds his or her position for life! However, it is

quite unusual for the president's selection not to be

confirmed by the Senate.

21st Century Content

Most of the countries in the world have some type of Supreme Court. Most also have local courts. The biggest difference is how judges are chosen—elected or appointed, perhaps by the king or a "Supreme Council".

All the justices of the Supreme Court were white males until
Thurgood Marshall, an African American, joined the court in 1967.

The Supreme Court deals with interpreting the laws of the United

States. This comes in the form of a court case, in which there is a

disagreement about the meaning of a law. Such a court case usually takes

many years to reach the Supreme Court. The case must be taken to other, lower courts first. Once all of the lower

courts have spoken about the case, one side or the

other in the disagreement may submit it to the

Supreme Court.

The Supreme Court justices take their work very,

very seriously. Their decisions can affect the lives of

many Americans. The justices hear cases and meet

to discuss them. Then they vote. One justice writes a

report to explain their decision. Other justices may

write about the case, too. Sometimes the Supreme

Court rules that a law is unconstitutional. If they

decide this, then the law is no longer in effect.

Sandra Day O'Connor was the first female justice. Although she got very good grades, she had trouble getting a job when she first got out of law school. How did perseverance help her in life?

The Supreme Court Building was completed in 1935. It contains private offices for each justice, a courtroom, and a library, among other areas.

If the Supreme Court declares a law to be

unconstitutional, Congress may decide to rewrite

the law to fix the problem. If this happens, Congress

will go through all the steps again, and the president

will have to sign the bill into law again. This is the

wonderful system that the Founding Fathers created.

No one of the three branches has the power to be a

tyrant. All three must work together to create good

laws for all Americans.

Why would leadership and ethics be good qualities for a Supreme Court justice?

GLOSSARY

amendments (uh-MEND-muhnts) changes to a constitution or other official document

appropriations (uh-proh-pree-EY-shuhns) Congressional decisions on how money should be distributed

bill (bil) name for a proposed law

direct democracy (di-REKT di-MOK-ruh-see) one in which all citizens vote on every issue

executive (ig-ZEK-yuh-tiv) branch of the federal government that is headed by the president

hearings (HEER-ingz) meetings in Congress where members listen to the views of experts and citizens

House of Representatives (hous uv rep-ri-ZEN-tuh-tivz) one of the two parts of Congress

judicial (joo-DISH-uhl) branch of the federal government that is made up of the court system

legislative (LEJ-is-ley-tiv) branch of the federal government that is made up of Congress

override (oh-ver-RAHYD) vote in Congress to create a law after a president has turned it down

representative democracy (rep-ri-ZEN-tuh-tiv di-MOK-ruh-see) one in which citizens elect others to represent them in the decision-making process

Senate (SEN-it) one of the two parts of Congress

separation of powers (sep-uh-REY-shuhn uv POU-erz) division of power among the three branches of the federal government

tyrant (TAHY-ruhnt) ruler who governs, often unfairly, without any restrictions

unconstitutional (uhn-kon-sti-TOO-shuh-nl) something that goes against the United States Constitution

veto (VEE-toh) refuse approval

For More Information

Books

Editors of Time. *Benjamin Franklin: A Man of Many Talents.*
New York: Harper Trophy, 2005.

Krull, Kathleen. *A Kids' Guide to America's Bill of Rights:
Curfews, Censorship, and the 100-Pound Giant.*
New York: HarperCollins, 1999.

Maestro, Betsy. *A More Perfect Union: The Story of Our Constitution.*
New York: Harper Trophy, 1990.

Sobel, Syl. *The U.S. Constitution and You.*
Hauppauge, NY: Barron's Educational Series, 2001.

Soble, Syl. *How the U.S. Government Works.*
Hauppauge, NY: Barron's Educational Series, 1999.

Other Media

American Experience: TR, The Story of Theodore Roosevelt.
DVD. PBS Home Video, 1996.

American Experience: One Woman, One Vote.
DVD. PBS Home Video, 1995.

The Congress. DVD. PBS Home Video, 1989.

Declaration of Independence. DVD. The History Channel, 2005.

The Presidents. DVD. The History Channel, 2005.

Sandra Day O'Connor. DVD. The History Channel.

To find out more about how a bill becomes a law, go to
http://clerkkids.house.gov/laws/index.html

To find out more about presidential vetoes, go to
http://clerk.house.gov/art_history/house_history/vetoes.html

INDEX

ABOUT THE AUTHOR

Fredrik Liljeblad is a professional writer and the author of many books and articles on subjects as varied as languages, politics, movies, and travel. He has lived in many countries, including Japan, Thailand, Taiwan, Sweden, England, and now lives in Southern California with his two cats, Smoky and Gombei. His main hobby is gardening—especially roses and camellias—and he often writes about gardening for magazines.